SHIPS ON THE HUMBER

Captain John Hood

at heart ♡ publications
www.atheart.co.uk

First published in 2008 by
At Heart Ltd
32 Stamford Street
Altrincham
Cheshire
WA14 1EY

ISBN: 978-1-84547-214-6

Printed and bound by Ashford Colour Press, Gosport.

For my dear and long-suffering wife, Rosemary.

Cover image

Cometa passing the Grimsby Dock Tower, 26 July 2001.

Acknowledgements

This book would not have been possible without the help of many people.

Firstly I must thank Bernard Bale who took my quip about ship photographs seriously and worked so hard to provide a platform from which it could be launched.

I must also include my son-in-law, Stef Milano, for his technical help and assistance in research.

Then there are all those with whom I have had the pleasure of working on the River Humber. My fellow Berthing Masters at the Tetney Monobuoy and the management of Tetney Oil Terminal all showed a wonderful tolerance of my desire to take my camera with me wherever I went.

The crew and skippers of the work boats, *Spurn Haven II* and *Monogirl*, especially merit my thanks for the way they have accommodated my desires to 'get a little closer' to a certain vessel. Without them it couldn't have been done and there would be no book. Indeed, my grateful thanks to all those I have worked with over these past 30 years. I hope you think it was worth it!

Foreword

I first came to work on the River Humber in 1978 and I am still here 30 years later, albeit in a part-time capacity.

I was employed for 25 years as a Berthing Master at the Tetney Monobuoy working for Conoco (now ConocoPhillips).

I soon began taking photographs of tankers coming to the monobuoy simply as a kind of record keeping, but I expanded by taking photographs of other types of vessels until I have reached the stage where, now, if it floats I photograph it!

In compiling this book I had two objectives in mind. For those who have worked in the Humber Estuary and Lower Humber areas, I hope it serves as a pleasant reminder of the ships which have passed through over the years. For those who do not know the River Humber, I hope that the book shows the variety of shipping that is found there and the pleasure that can be gained from photographing it.

The Humber Estuary is remarkable!

It drains 28 per cent of England and is one of the most dangerous rivers in the world to navigate.

Every tide 100,000 tonnes of silt move in and out of the estuary; every year 60 million tonnes of cargo move on its waters and every year 1 million passengers embark or disembark at one of its ports.

Naturally, such a vibrant waterway gives rise to a huge variety of shipping using it.

In this book I hope you will find a fair representation of that variety of shipping.

That variety includes Hull trawlers, Grimsby 'Snibbies', a plethora of Ro-Ros and Car Carriers together with sea/river vessels, coasters of all shapes and sizes as well as small work boats and tugs, dredgers, dive support vessels and specialized ships of all sorts.

I have also tried to include vessels of interest. An example of this is the 1957-built Port Line ship, now unrecognisable, or the 1958 Bowater vessel that just goes on and on! A tug capsize during a routine berthing operation is both dangerous and memorable; in this book you see the evidence.

Which was the most expensive oil tanker ever built? This book has the answer... and the photograph! I have been fortunate enough to photograph what must be almost the last examples of real 'ship shape ships'. Hence, the book includes photographs of ships with derricks and 'old fashioned' heavy lift gear.

I have spent all my working life on ships and love them. My hope is that this book helps you to see them the same way.

Captain John Hood

Evita

72,120 grt
126,352 dwt

Designed to operate in the difficult weather and sea conditions in the northern sector of the North Sea, the twin-screw *Evita* was built by the Dalian Shipyard, Dalian, China, for AS Ugland Shuttle Tanker Co, Grimstad, Norway. Completed in 1989, the Evita is 260m loa; 46m in the beam, and capable of 14 knots.

By 2000, Ugland Capital Parners were operating a number of similar vessels. The 1986-built *Nordic Sarita* (ex *Sarita*) and the 1990s-built *Stena Alexita* and *Stena Sinita* were with Interocean Ugland Management Services AS. As well as *Evita*, Ugland Marine Services AS had built *Juanita* (ex *Lisita*) and the Canadian-registered *Kometik* and *Mattea*. This last pair were both completed in 1997; *Kometic* was managed by Canship Ugland for Mobil Oil while *Mattea* was owned by Canship Ltd. The picture shows *Evita* approaching the Tetney Monobuoy on a fine day in June 1994.

Nordica

4,800 dwt

Described as a multi-functional vessel based on an ice-breaker design, *Nordica* can also deploy ploughing and trenching machines as well as tow or operate as a supply ship. Built in 1994, she is owned by Fintaship of Finland and is registered in Helsinki. She made a brief visit to the Humber Estuary on 10 July 1995 to take on stores and change crew.

Endeavour

9,963 grt

Photographed against the rising sun on 4 July 1995, *Endeavour* is seen in the Bull Channel on passage for Immingham Dock. Built in 1976 by Porsgrund Mekaniske, Verksted, Norway, for Fred Olsen Seaspeed Ferries, she has had seven different owners and seven changes of name. When photographed, she was owned by Exxtor Ferries of Immingham.

Polyviking

73,935 grt
130,700 dwt

Owned by Einar Rasmussen, Kristiansand, Norway, *Polyviking* was the first specifically built North Sea Shuttle Tanker, and had been designed to meet the requirements for loading crude oil from the Norwegian Statfjord Oil Field.

Built by Uddevallavarvet AB, Uddevalla, Sweden, and completed in 1983, *Polyviking* cost so much money – she was the most expensive tanker ever built – that she was nicknamed the *Queen of the North Sea*. She is seen here approaching Tetney Monobuoy on 2 March 1995. In 1998 she became the *Navion Viking*, owned by Rasmussen-Navion KS; a joint venture with the Navion shipping division of Norwegian Government controlled Statoil AS.

Bregen
10,012 grt
13,941 dwt

The coastal chemical tanker *Bregen* in ballast condition in the Bull Anchorage on 24 May 1999, awaiting berthing instructions for Salt End. At the time, *Bregen* was the smallest vessel in the Bergshav Management AS fleet, and their only twin-screw ship.

At the other end of the scale was the *Svelik*, at 134164 grt, 276100 dwt, 341m loa, beam 54m, and driven by steam turbines. Dating from 1975, she was the oldest vessel in the fleet.

Bregen was built in 1994 by the Ching Fu Shipbuilding Co Ltd, Kaohsuing, Taiwan. She measured 150m loa, beam 21m, and was capable of 13 knots.

Hendrik-B
3,210 grt

A geared twin-hatch general cargo vessel seen in the Humber Estuary on 24 May 1999 which was, apparently, a somewhat hazy day! The ship was built in 1982 as the *Polarborg* but changed name in 1995. She was built by Nieuwe Noord Nederlandse Scheepswerven, Groningen and is owned by Wagenborg Shipping.

Dana Cimbria
12,189 grt

Ro-Ro ferry, *Dana Cimbria*, was owned and operated by the Danish company, DFDS Scandinavian Seaways, which is now DFDS Tor Line. She was built in 1986 by Frederikshavn Vaerft AS, Frederikshavn. She is seen here on 3 December 2000, at the seaward end of the Bull Channel approaching Spurn Point, outwards from Immingham Dock to Cuxhaven.

Puccini
2,195 grt
3,052 dwt

A chemical/product tanker managed by GEFO, Gesellschaft fur Oeltransporte mbH, she was built in 1998 by the Damien Shipyard BV. She is owned by Oceanflag Shipping. Seen on 14 December 2000 in ballast in the Bull Anchorage she is waiting for a berth at either Immingham Oil Terminal or Salt End.

Danubegas
4,000 dwt

A fine looking, colourful and photogenic LPG tanker owned by the German company Hartmann-Reederi and completed in 1998 by Sevenau SA, Turnu Severin, Romania. *Danubegas* is seen here in the Bull Anchorage on a fine sunny day, 20 November 2000, awaiting a berth at the Immingham Oil Terminal.

Putford Sea Mussell
865 grt

Putford Sea Mussell is an offshore standby vessel used to provide safety and rescue services to oil rigs and production platforms in the North Sea. She is owned by Boston Putford Offshore Safety Ltd and was acquired by them in 1993. Built as a supply vessel, she was modified in 1993 and again in 1998. Seen at the western end of the Bull Anchorage on 20 November 2000 waiting for stores and a crew change before resuming offshore duties.

Pascale Knutsen
11,688 grt
14,848 dwt

Owned by Knutsen OAS Shipping AS of Havgasund, Norway, the *Pascale Knutsen* is a regular visitor to the Immingham Oil Terminal. This chemical/oil product tanker was completed by Juliana Constroctora Gijonesa, Gijon, Spain in 1993 and is one of a number of vessels of similar dimensions in the Knutsen fleet; 142m loa, beam 23m, single-screw capable of 13 knots. Others include the *Ellen Knutsen* and *Synnove Knutsen*, both of which were completed in 1992 and are operated by JO Tankers. Then there is the *Helene Knutsen* (built 1992), *Torril Knutsen* (1990) and the *Turid Knutsen* (1993).

RNLI
Pride of the Humber

The RNLI took delivery of this Severn Class lifeboat in 1997 for use on the permanently manned Lifeboat Station on Spurn Point. Brian Bevan was the coxwain for many years, during which time he became one of the most decorated lifeboatmen ever. This class of lifeboat was introduced in 1995 and had a top speed of 25 knots. She is seen here on a training exercise, on 18 April 2001, in the Bull Fort/Haille Channel area of the Lower Humber.

Inge   The *Inge* was a locally owned tug operating out of Grimsby. She was built in 1962 as the *Stedington* and was bought in 1995 by Captain I.R. Harvey of Grimsby. She finds employment assisting with the berthing of the many car carriers using Grimsby as well as transporting crew, stores and fresh water to ships anchored in the estuary. She was photographed on 18 April 2001 in Grimsby Roads waiting to assist with the berthing of a car carrier.

Norse Mersey

15,000 grt

For a few years this Ro-Ro ferry was a regular visitor to Immingham while on charter to DFDS as part of the Immingham–Rotterdam service. Her distinctive colour scheme made her stand out among the blues and greys usually associated with Ro-Ro shipping on the Humber. She was built in 1995 by Visentini, Donada.

She is seen here on 2 March 2001 in the vicinity of the East Chequer Light Float. She is embarking a pilot, indicating that her master did not possess a Pilotage Exemption Certificate.

Estoril

5,222 grt
1,400 dwt

Another unlovely but useful vessel. Built in 1974 at Harfleur Shipyard ACH, le Havre, *Estoril* was owned by United European Car Carriers and had a capacity of 600 cars.

She was a regular visitor to the Alexandra Dock, Grimsby, bringing cars manufactured by VAG and taking out British-made Rovers and Toyotas. She was photographed on 2 March 2001 entering the seaward end of the Bull Channel, on passage for Grimsby.

Tor Futura

18,469 grt

Completed at Donada, Italy, in 1996, *Tor Futura* is the only one of the Tor Line ferries where any attempt was made at streamlining the funnel. In this picture, the vessel is outward from Immingham on 2 March 2001 and has just passed Spurn Point.

By this date DFDS and Tor Line had amalgamated to form DFDS Tor Line, and in January 2002 the new company acquired a 66 per cent stake in the Norwegian container line Lys-Line which at the time owned eight side-loading Ro-Ro and container ships, and had another ten on charter. DFDS had already acquired the Lithuanian company, Lisco.

Moyallon
18.4 grt

An excellent example of a wooden Girvan-built fishing vessel, *Moyallon* was built in 1985. She was photographed on 14 March 2001 in Grimsby Roads, having just left Grimsby Fish Dock.

Audacity
3,780 dwt

One of Fred Everard's fleet, the motor tanker *Audacity* is seen here in the Humber Estuary on 31 March 2001 approaching the Bull Anchorage to find a spot while awaiting a berth at the Immingham Oil Terminal. She was built at Keppel Singmarine Dockyard in 1997.

This fully automated coastal product tanker sparked off a search and rescue mission on the evening of 16 June 2005 when she came upon an upturned dinghy 15 miles off Sheringham. The Sheringham lifeboat, which was already at sea on an exercise, was able to respond quickly.

The dinghy – named *Warthog* – had a broken mast but her sails were set. The lifeboatmen also came across lifejackets and a bag containing personal effects. The search would involve the Cromer and Wells all-weather lifeboats a RAF helicopter, a couple of US helicopters that happened to be on an exercise nearby, the Wells in-shore lifeboat and the Hunstanton and Wells Coastguard Rescue Teams. In response to a general VHF call, the rig *Glamar Labrador* offered its services as a communications centre and a number of ships including *Stena Searider*, *Union Topaz*, *Nora Wilson*, and *Havila Sun* joined in.

At first light, the Coastguard Rescue Teams searched the shoreline, and by the time the search ended at 0830hrs, it had been established that *Warthog* had sailed from Wells three days earlier bound for Brancaster. It appeared that her occupant, a man, had no radio aboard.

Asperity
3,780 dwt

The *Asperity*, entering the Bull Anchorage in ballast with Spurn Point in the background on 25 January 2000.

Double-hull coastal product tanker built for F.T. Everard, London, in 1997 by Keppel Singmarine Pte Ltd and now owned by James Fisher Everard of Barrow in Furness. Sistership of *Audacity*, *Asperity* is seen here in ballast on 4 March 2001. She is in the Bull Anchorage awaiting a berth at the Immingham Oil Terminal.

Rix Condor

827 grt
1,240 dwt

Built in 1967, at more than 41 years old she looks to be wearing well and in good condition. The term 'Bunker Barge' hardly seems suitable but her present role is one of a bunkering vessel.

Her present owners are Rix Shipping and she is regularly seen in the Humber. She is shown loaded and awaiting orders in the Bull Anchorage on 18 March 2001.

Galwad-y-mor

22 grt

A Southampton-registered fishing vessel built in 1984 at Mevagissey, *Galwad-y-mor* is seen on 14 March 2001 in Grimsby Roads after leaving Grimsby Fish Dock for sea.

Ingeborg Pilot
1,196 grt
1,053 dwt

Ingeborg Pilot is pictured in the Humber Estuary on 14 March 2001, in what appears to loaded condition, outwards from one of the upriver ports on the Trent or Ouse. She is owned by Norbroker Shipping & Transport and was built in 1981. She is another good example of the modern, versatile single-hatch coaster.

Spruce
7,258 grt

A barge carrier like the *Spruce* is an unusual vessel in any estuary. The official description is Lighter Aboard Ship (LASH ship). She has large ballast tanks on each side (the port side ones are easily visible in the picture) which she fills to bring the cargo area down to water level. The barges can then be floated out and towed to wherever required. Each barge is 385 tonnes, and the *Spruce* has capacity for 85 of them. She was built in 1975 by Sumitomo Heavy Industries, Tokyo. The angled boom towards the stern of the vessel acts as a support for the after steaming light.

Tarnfjord
19,990 dwt

A fine example of a well-maintained Swedish owned product tanker, *Tarnfjord* was built in 1984 by Kaldnes Mekaniske Verksted, Tonsberg. She is owned and operated by Tärntank Rederi AB, Sweden. A regular visitor to the Immingham Oil Terminal, she is seen here on 12 March 2001 crossing the Bull Anchorage to a designated position to await a berth.

Pointe Du Crosic

An LPG tanker. Owned by Eitzen Gas AS, Denmark, she was built in 2001 by Aker Yards, Floro AS. This photograph, taken on 7 March 2001 shows the vessel in the bull Anchorage with Spurn Pilot Station on Spurn Point in the background.

Putford Sky
428 grt

Putford Sky is a standby/safety vessel used to provide safety and rescue services for the oil rigs and production platforms in the North Sea. She was built by Brooke Marine of Lowestoft in 1967 and was launched as the *Dawn Sky*. Her owners, Boston Putford Offshore Safety Ltd, bought her in 1994. She is registered in Lowestoft, and seen here on 4 March 2001 at the western end of the Bull Anchorage waiting for stores and a change of crew.

Autoracer
9,693 grt

Autoracer is a United European Car Carrier's vessel built at Brattvaag Skipsverft (Norway) in 1994. This photograph was taken on 26 July 2001 showing the ship at Freshney Wharfe in the Alexandra Dock, Grimsby. She appears to be floating on a sea of cars and vans! She was one of a new breed of car carrier built for UECC and was capable of 20 knots fully laden.

Sundaberg
2,385 grt

A Faroese-registered fish factory vessel, seen here on 26 July 2001 crossing Grimsby Royal Dock to her berth ready to discharge a cargo of fish and fish products. The Cod War brought about great changes and here we see the evidence! Nonetheless, a fine looking ship and well worthy of a photograph. She is owned by JFK of Klaksvic, Faroe Islands, and was built in 1988. She fishes in the Barents Sea and the East Greenland Sea.

Cometa
4,610 grt

Although the *Cometa* may not look like the average geared feeder container vessel that is what she is. For as long as most people can remember, she has been on a regular run between Norway and Grimsby with containers. She berths in Grimsby Royal Dock and handles the containers with her own special crane. The ship lists alarmingly when lowering the container to the dock side, but the length of time it has been going on shows what a safe operation this is.

The photograph was taken on 26 July 2001 and shows the *Cometa* traversing Grimsby Royal Dock towards her regular berth, with the famous Grimsby Dock Tower in the background. She was built in 1981 by Fosen Mek Verksteder, Norway. She is owned by Sea Cargo AS of Bergen.

Laura

5,239 grt

A feeder container vessel owned by Oy JIT-Trans Ltd, Raahe, Finland, *Laura* was on one of her regular runs to Hull when pictured lying at the northern edge of the Bull Anchorage on 23 July 2001. JIT-Trans provides container services between many British and near European ports.

Autofreighter

5,927 grt

Grimsby is such a large car import and export port that numerous vehicle carriers feature in this book. No apologies, then, for including this fairly early example, built in 1977 at Capelle. She carries 580 cars at a speed of 12.5 knots. She is owned by United European Car Carriers of Oslo. Unusually, she has twin propellers. This photograph, taken on 23 July 2001, shows her picking up speed, outward bound from Grimsby in the Bull Channel.

Elisebeth   A good example of a sea/river coaster entering the Bull Anchorage from sea to await a berth. The photograph, taken on 6 April 2001, indicates that *Elisebeth* is carrying a cargo of timber so she may have been bound for Grimsby, Barrow or New Holland. The lettering on the side shows that she was under charter to Echoship APS of Svendborg, Denmark.

Dutch Faith
4,425 dwt

Shown here on 6 April 2001 passing Spurn Point, outward bound from Salt End Jetty. Together with her sister vessels, *Dutch Faith* was a regular visitor to the Humber for many years. She is a sophisticated Type 2 stainless steel chemical tanker. She was built in 1996 at Shipyard De Hoop in the Netherlands for the GB Shipping Service BV, Dordrecht.

Ernest Shackleton
4,028 grt

Properly described as the Royal Research Ship *Ernest Shackleton*, she was built in 1995 by Kverner Klevin Leirvik AS, Norway as the *Polar Queen*. The British Antarctic Survey acquired her on a long-term charter in 1999. She replaced the RRS Bransfield.

She is registered at Stanley in the Falkland Isles. The picture shows her in Grimsby Royal Dock on 30 April 2001 unloading after her annual trip to the Antarctic. For the northern summer she is employed in various aspects of commercial survey work in the North Sea area.

Donnington
5,351 grt

A vehicle carrier owned by United European Car Carriers of Oslo, she was built in 1976 as the *Tertre Rouge* by the Société des Chantiers de Graville. She was bought by UECC in 1989 and became the *Donnington*. She is seen here in the Bull Channel on 30 April 2001, inwards for the Alexandra Dock, Grimsby, via the 'level' in the Royal Dock lock.

Wilson Rhine

1,171 grt
1,832 dwt

Owned by Wilson Ship Management AS, the
Wilson Rhine waits at the eastern end of the
Bull Anchorage for discharge orders on 21 July
2001. She was built in 1998 by Ceskoslovenska
Plavba Labska AS, and is registered at
Bridgetown, Barbados.

CSO Orelia

Launched at Swan Hunter on 11 December 1982, the diving support vessel *Orelia* was completed in 1984 for Houlder Offshore Ltd. Her unusual design gives 'low roll' characteristics and allows her to operate in most weather and sea states. Her sophisticated dynamic positioning system is capable of holding her steady above a well-head via computer controls to her Mirrlees engines, double-reduction geared to three shafts. She is seen here passing Spurn Point on 21 July 2001, en route for diving operations in the North Sea.

Transcarrier
8,476 grt

For a short period this Ro-Ro was a regular visitor to Grimsby under a Sea-Cargo charter which required her to berth stern to the west side of Grimsby Royal Dock, effectively blocking the dock. She is seen here in the Bull Anchorage on 20 March 2001. She was built in 1994 by Kraljevica Shipyard, Rijeka. Registered in Nassau, she is owned by Valmue Shipping KS, Bergen.

Tor Britannia
21,491 grt

This one of a number of similar vessels providing a Ro-Ro service from Immingham to near European ports before the advent of what we might call the 'super Ro-Ro'. She is seen here on 8 March 1997 in the Humber Estuary, outward bound from Immingham Dock. She was built by Soc Metallurgique & Navale Dunkerque–Normandie, Dunkirk in 1978 as the *Ville du Havre*. Over the years she experienced a number of name changes, until she was lengthened in 1994 and became *Tor Britannia*. She has since been sold by Tor Line.

Tor Britannia

24,196 grt

This *Tor Britannia* was a familiar Ro-Ro operating on the Immingham–near Europe run. She is seen in the photograph on 21 July 2001 in the Bull Channel, outwards from Immingham. She was operated by DFDS Tor Line, owned by DFDS AS and registered in Kobenhavn. The vessel is a good example of the new breed of Ro-Ro brought in to replace aging tonnage in the late 1990s. She was built in 2000 by Fincantieri, Cantieri Navali.

Finnmaster

Another colourful addition to the Ro-Ro vessels using the Humber Estuary, *Finnmaster* was owned by Nordic Holdings and was then being operated by Finncarriers as shown by the logo on her side. She is seen on 27 August 2001 just approaching Spurn Point on her outward passage. The vessel was a product of the Chinese Jinling Shipyard being built in 2000.

Hanne Knutsen

71,850 grt
126,000 dwt

The 15-knot twin-screw *Hanne Knutsen* is a splendid example of a second generation North Sea Shuttle Tanker. Completed in 2000 by Asterilleros de Sestao, SRL, Spain, for Knutsen OAS Shipping AS of Norway, she is 165m loa with a beam of 43m. She is seen here in the Humber Estuary on 27 August 2001 approaching the Tetney Monobuoy.

Steersman

4,942 grt
6,403 dwt

One of three 6,000-tonne vessels owned by James Fisher Tankships Ltd, Steersman was built in 1994 by the Malaysia Shipyard & Engineering Co, Johor. Her sisters are the *Chartsman* (6,397 dwt) and the *Rudderman* (6,418 dwt). These vessels are 101.6m loa and have a beam of 17.5m. Powered by the Mirrlees ESL 16 MKII 3,550bhp engine, they are capable of 12.5 knots and are also equipped with the Schottel bow thruster. *Steersman* is pictured here crossing the Bull Anchorage on 20 March 2001 to await loading orders.

Annuity

3,294 dwt

Built in 1988, *Annuity* was the class name for a new style of chemical tanker built for F.T. Everard of London. The vessel was built by Nordsovaeftet, Ringkobing and is now owned by the joint venture: James Fisher Everard. In the photograph she is shown in the Humber Estuary on 31 March 2001, inwards for Salt End Jetty.

Swanella
1,195 grt

A famous name in the J. Marr & Sons trawler fleet, the *Swanella*, pictured here on 2 March 2001, was built in 1989 by Slipen Mek Verksted AS, Norway, as the *Stamsund*. She saw service under Norwegian, French and Icelandic colours prior to being registered in the UK. In 2008 she was registered in Russia. She is seen here on 2 March 2001 on passage from the fishing grounds to Hull to discharge her catch.

John Biscoe   *John Biscoe* is seen here alongside the old coal berth in Grimsby Royal Dock during her summer lay up in June 1982. Every year she would return to the UK during the Antarctic winter, dry-dock on the Tyne and then lay up and replenish stores and crew in Grimsby ready for the trip south in early September.

She was built by Flemming & Ferguson of Paisley in 1956 and was registered at Stanley in the Falkland Islands. She was operated by the British Antarctic Survey from 1956 until 1991 when she was replaced by the *James Clark Ross*. The *John Biscoe* was sold and became the *Fayza Express*. She was scrapped in 2004.

Surrey
3,375 grt

Pictured in July 1984 manoeuvring out of the Royal Dock, Grimsby, with the assistance of the tug, *Lady Elizabeth*. *Surrey* was built in 1969 by Helsingor Skibsværft og Maskinbyggeri AIS, Elsinore. She was owned by the Danish operator, DFDS Seaways, and was on a regular service from Grimsby to Esbjerg until 1992 when she was replaced. She was later renamed *Patra*, and then *Pit* when she was sold in 1999. The *Lady Elizabeth* was built in 1981 by Cochrane Shipbuilders of Selby and owned by Howard Smith Towage. With a bollard pull of 32 tonnes, she is a useful harbour tug.

Shearwater Topaz
3,963 grt

Shearwater Topaz is a 1983-built dive support vessel owned by the Lyle Offshore Group. The ship is pictured in March 1984, secured to a four-point mooring off Tetney Monobuoy to provide a platform for diving operations to replace the sub-sea hose connecting the buoy to the seabed PLEM. She was built by the De Hoop Shipyard, Holland and is registered in that country.

Norland

26,290 grt (after lengthening)

In the Humber Estuary, outward bound from Hull to Zeebrugge on the evening 4 May 1984. She is shown here in the original North Sea ferry colour scheme. The vessel was built in 1973 by A.G. Weser, Werk Seebeck, Bremerhaven.

In March 1982 she was requisitioned as a troopship for use in the Falklands Task Force. She returned to Hull in February 1983 and was back in service that same year. In 1987 she went back to A.G. Weser of Bremerhaven to be lengthened. At the same time, North Sea Ferries changed their colour scheme. She is in the Humber Estuary heading for sea and the crossing to Zeebrugge.

The lengthened *Norland* in the Bull Channel on the evening 3 July 1994, heading for Zeebrugge.

Dana Maxima
13,303 grt
17,068 grt (after lengthening)

Photographed on the evening of 5 August 1990, the *Dana Maxima* is seen in the Bull Channel on passage from Grimsby to Esbjerg. The picture shows the ferry in the original DFDS colours and gives an idea of what she looked like before she was lengthened in 1995. She was built by Hitachi Zosen, Osaka, Japan in 1978 and delivered direct to DFDS for the Grimsby–Esbjerg service.

Dana Maxima, seen here in the colours of DFDS Transport in the Bull Channel on 8 August 1997, outwards from Immingham to Esbjerg. In 1995 she was lengthened, meaning that she could no longer use Grimsby; hence the move to Immingham.

Helmsman
6,165 dwt

Seen in this photograph on 5 June 1992, anchored in the Bull Anchorage, some two years before being sold. *Helmsman* was built in 1972 by Cochrane & Sons Ltd, Selby and thus enjoyed a sideways launch. Initially the owner was C. Rowbotham. & Sons (Management) Ltd, a family-owned business which was a powerful force in the coastal tanker trade. This continued until 1993 when the company was taken over by P&O Tankships Ltd. In 1994 she was sold to Galana Petroleum Ltd, Kenya and renamed *Rufiji*.

Spurn Haven
262 grt
192 dwt

Spurn Haven was built in 1966, as one of the first North Sea Supply Ships by J. Lewis & Sons Ltd of Aberdeen. By modern standards she was very small. In 1970 she was bought by Spurn Shipping & Co Ltd, Grimsby, for use as a Monobuoy Support Vessel. Her name was changed from *Lady Edwina* to *Spurn Haven*. In 1976 she was sold to Conoco Ltd and continued to be a familiar sight in the estuary until 1994 when Conoco sold her. The photograph shows her just off the Bull Fort in July 1992.

Audrey   Seen here under a good set of sails in the Bull Channel, *Audrey* was a steel hulled, 60ft sailing barge. Registered in Goole, she was owned and operated by the Sobriety Project, a Goole charity aiming to take out parties of young offenders and disadvantaged youths. She was regularly seen in Grimsby and was photographed on 3 June 1992.

Lady Cecilia

Bollard pull: 52 tonnes

Lady Cecilia is seen here on 15 July 1992 assisting as 'stern tug' to a tanker secured to the Tetney Monobuoy, in the Humber Estuary. The tug was built in 1991 by McTay Marine of Bromborough and was owned by Howard Smith Towage at the time. She was one of a class of tug new to the Humber and one that has proved very successful both in docks and in the estuary. With a bollard pull of 52 tonnes via two Voith 32G - 11/200 propulsion units, she and her sisters have been useful in the Humber.

Spurn Haven II   Seen here in the Humber Estuary in July 1994, this vessel was originally built as a
Gulf of Mexico Supply Ship named the *Ventura*. She was bought by Conoco in 1992
for their monobuoy operation in the Humber Estuary and after extensive re-fitting at
Lowestoft came to the Humber in November 1993.

Monogirl   A Heavy Duty Mooring Launch seen here in the vicinity of Tetney Monobuoy in June 1994.
She was owned by Conoco Ltd and built in 1971 by N.V. Scheepswerf Schouten, Moiden
Holland. Conoco bought her in 1975 to relpace the *Jakoma*. She has a length of 50ft and
displaces 46 tonnes when loaded. She was still in service in June 2008.

Lady Moira

Bollard pull: 50 tonnes

When this photograph was taken, on 24 August 1994, *Lady Moira* was owned by Howard Smith Towage. She was built in 1978 by Cochrane Shipbuilders of Selby for Humber Tugs Ltd, and had a bollard pull provided by two 1,460bhp Rushton engines linked to twin fixed propellers in kort nozzles. Although used mainly in harbour and estuary work, she also operated extensively in coastal work and short sea voyages. She is seen here approaching the Tetney Monobuoy ready to assist with the berthing of a tanker at the buoy.

This second photograph of the *Lady Moira* provides an unpleasant reminder that things can go wrong in a routine berthing operation. On the morning of 6 June 1992, the Dutch Shell tanker *Sedalia* was scheduled to berth at Tetney Monobuoy at high water, about 1030hrs. *Lady Moira* was the stern tug and made fast as usual. However, during the process of swinging from the port quarter to an astern position the capsize occurred. The second tug, *Lady Anya*, was quickly on the scene as the photograph shows, ready to take off crew members in danger. The tanker quickly took her way off and *Lady Moira* resumed an upright position. Not surprisingly, the berthing was cancelled.

Ivybank

11,405 grt
15,216 dwt

Bank Line (Andrew Weir & Co Ltd) stands out as one of the greatest and longest lasting of Britain's shipping companies. In the early 1970s the company placed an order for six cargo liners for its Trans-Pacific services with Swan Hunter Shipbuilders Ltd. Of these, *Corabank*, *Moraybank*, and *Ivybank* were laid down at the Readhead yard, South Shields, which Swans had taken over in January 1968. *Ivybank* is seen here on 3 October 1994 in the Bull Channel, having recently sailed from Hull. By this date break-bulk cargo was almost a thing of the past, hence the containers on her deck. Still in good condition after 20 years' service, *Ivybank* would have another four to do in Bank Line colours before being sold to a St.Vincent based company and renamed *Pro Pacifica*.

Norsun

31,598 grt

On a summer evening in July 1994, *Norsun* makes her way down the Bull Channel, outward from Hull for the overnight crossing to Hook of Holland. She was built in 1987 by Nippon Kokan KK, Tsurumi, and was owned by North Sea Ferries when this picture was taken.

Pholas

4,045 grt

An unusual-looking vessel seen anchored in the
NE end of the Bull Anchorage in November
1994. Described as a Research / Soil Sampling
Vessel and owned at the time by Coe Metcalf
Shipping Ltd, the *Pholas* had a past. Those with
a keen eye will recognise her as none other than
Elizabeth Bowater, a pulp-carrying motorship
built by Caledon Shipbuilding & Engineering,
Dundee, in 1958 for the Bowater Steamship Co.
In 1972 she was sold to Wimpey (Marine) Ltd,
who converted her to a drill ship and remained
with them until purchased by Coe Metcalf in
1980, who renamed her *Pholas*. In 1998, she
was still in use by a Norwegian company.

River Andoni

10,985 grt
11,557 dwt

A fine-looking general cargo vessel which looks to have fallen on hard times! The *River Andoni* was one of a number of 10,985 grt, 147m loa, 23m beam, 16 knot motorships built in the late 1970s for the Nigerian National Shipping Line Ltd. Others included *River Asab*, *River Jimini*, *River Kerewa* and *River Mada*. Registered in Lagos, this product from Hyundai Heavy Industries Co Ltd, South Korea, spent her entire career with the NNSL before being sold for scrap in 1997. She was broken up at Aliaga, Turkey. This picture was taken in the Bull Anchorage on 23 January 1994, where she was awaiting orders having discharged at Hull.

Vikla   Here we see an ice-breaking chemical tanker at the west end of the Bull Channel, outwards from Salt End Jetty on 5 March 1995. The vessel was built in 1982 by the Vuossaari Shipyard in Helsinki, Finland and is a Super Ice Class Tanker. The funnel colours show the owner as Neste Oyj, the national oil company of Finland. In later years the shipping side of the company was passed to Fortum Shipping of Finland and, while the funnel colour changed to dark blue, the emblem remained much the same. In 2004 the vessel was sold to Polish interests.

Humber Surveyor   A beautiful wooden-built survey vessel owned by ABP and used for all marine survey work in the Humber Estuary and Upper and Lower Humber. She is seen here at the entrance to Grimsby Royal Dock on 15 May 1995.

TS Royalist   On 20 November 1995, the TS *Royalist* left Hull after a visit during one of her weekly cruises so she is seen here, under power, in the Bull Channel, heading out to sea. She is a steel-built Brig, launched in 1972 by Princess Anne and is owned and operated by the Sea Cadet Corps of the United Kingdom.

Bransfield
4,816 grt

Bransfield was built in 1970 by Robb Caledon Shipbuilders Ltd of Leith for the British Antarctic Survey. Before the southern winter set in, the *Bransfield* would return to the UK for dry docking on the Tyne and lay up for stores and crew replenishment in Grimsby. Here she is seen alongside the east side, Grimsby Royal Dock in June 1995. She was registered in Stanley, Falkland Islands. She served the BAS until 1999 when she was sold to Reiber Shipping AS as part of the contract for the charter of the RRS, *Ernest Shackleton*.

Smolny
8,718 grt
11,760 dwt

Here is a break-bulk general cargo vessel of traditional style built in 1967 by Ga B-41/D2, Gdynia for the Polskie Towarzystwo Okretowe (Polish Shipping Association) fleet and was owned by Polskie Linie Oceaniczne (Polish Ocean Lines). She is seen here in deep-laden condition at the NE end of the Bull Anchorage; her deck cargo for discharge at Hull. *Smolny* served Polish Ocean Lines until sold for breaking up.

Lackenby

Having discharged her cargo of bulk iron ore at the Immingham Bulk Terminal, the *Lackenby* proceeds down the Bull Channel in May 1995, outwards for South Africa again, and with another cargo to feed the Scunthorpe steel works.

New Generation
2,355 grt

The carriage of heavy lift cargo makes an interesting study, and here we have a vessel specially built for the role. Built as the *Kingsnorth Fisher* in 1966, by the Ailsa Shipbuilding Co of Troon for James Fisher & Sons, Barrow, she was chartered by the CEGB for moving heavy components for power stations. She is seen here in the Bull Channel in May 1996.

Canlap Ikaluk
3,227 grt

On 8 November 1995 this powerful-looking offshore supply/safety vessel was powering up the Bull Channel towards Immingham. She was built in 1983 and is registered in Nassau. She is owned by Canmar.

Wellington Royal Air Force Marine Section *Spitfire* Class rescue and target towing launch, *Wellington*, is seen here making for Grimsby in July 1996. The class, built by James and Stone, Brightlingsea, were all named after World War Two aircraft. They displaced 70.2 tons, were 24.1m loa with a beam of 5.5m. Each was equipped with two Paxman engines and capable of a top speed of 22 knots. *Wellington* and *Hampden* provided cover for RAF and UASF aircraft using the bombing ranges near Donna Nook, on the south shore of the Humber Estuary.

Switzerland
15,833 grt

A lovely cruise liner passing Spurn Point on the evening of 8 May 1997, having embarked her passengers in Hull. Who, on seeing this photograph, could believe that the vessel dates from 1955? She was built by Swan Hunter & Wigham Richardson at Wallsend-on-Tyne as the 9,992 grt refrigerated cargo liner, *Port Sydney*, for Port Line's Australian meat trade. By the early 1970s, trade to Australia and New Zealand was bad enough for the *Port Sydney* to be laid up, pending sale. She was eventually bought by Greek interests Chion Shipping, who planned to convert her into a ferry, *Akrotiri Express*. However, before that happened, and after spending $30m, she was converted into a cruise liner. The 11683 grt *Daphne* made her maiden cruise in July 1975 for Costa Armatori SpA.

In 1997 she was taken over by Leisure Cruises of Switzerland, who aptly renamed her *Switzerland*. By 2007, she had undergone many changes in name and ownership: *Port Sydney*, *Akrotiri Express*, *Daphne*, *Switzerland*, *Ocean Odyssey* and *Ocean Monarch* owned by Majestic International Cruises. She is unlikely to survive much longer as the SOLAS 2010 regulations will mean the end of many older ships. These new regulations relate primarily to the use of combustible materials on cruise ships, and affects all ships built before 1974. One of the reasons for the withdrawal of the *QE2* was the prohibitive cost of bringing the vessel into line with the regulations in time for the introduction on 1 October 2010.

RNLI Kenneth Thelwall

The oil tycoon Mr Kenneth Thelwall of Beverley, associated with Thelson's Oil, East Yorkshire, died in 1986, leaving £3m to the RNLI in his will. The provision was that it should be spent on a new lifeboat together with its ancillary equipment. The result was the Arun Class lifeboat, *Kenneth Thelwall*, which was the Spurn Lifeboat until 1997. She was the RNLI's first UK designed 'fast lifeboat'. She displaced 31.5 tonnes and had a top speed of 18 knots. The lifeboat is seen in this photograph, taken on 8 March 1997, dressed overall and ready to be replaced by the present lifeboat, the *Pride of the Humber*.

RNLI City of Sheffield

This RNLI lifeboat is a modified Tyne Class which cost £500,000 in 1987. She began service as the Hartlepool Lifeboat, then was transferred to Whitby and now is stationed at Poole in Dorset. This photograph shows her in Grimsby Roads after leaving Grimsby Fish Docks on 7 April 1997.

Crusader (SH 173)
19.69 grt

Looking resplendent, with a newly painted hull and immaculately varnished wheelhouse, *Crusader* is a prime example of the type of inshore fishing vessel which used to frequent Grimsby Fish Dock after the demise of the deep water trawler fleet. Her registration, SH 173, shows her to be registered in Scarborough. She was built at Seahouses in 1969 and is seen here in Grimsby Roads, having just left Grimsby Fish Dock on 13 March 1997.

Kilgas Crusader
2,284 grt

Waiting in the Bull Anchorage for a berth at Immingham Gas Terminal is this colourful and, when this picture was taken on 15 August 1997, new vessel. Built in 1996, she very soon experienced a name change to *Sigas Crusader* and was owned by Eitzen Gas AS, Denmark. She is registered in Singapore.

Greenpeace

1,176 grt (when new)

Greenpeace is shown here on the east side of Grimsby Royal Dock on 7 April 1997. The vessel was built in 1959 as an ocean going tug/salvage vessel. In 1977, the vessel was converted and used as a Pilot Cutter until Greenpeace bought her in 1985. More alterations were made, and in 1986 she took over from the *Rainbow Warrior*, which had been sunk. She was registered in Amsterdam.

Ullswater
7,678 dwt

On a grey July day in 1997 the *Ullswater* lies at anchor in the Bull Anchorage waiting for a berth at the Immingham Gas Terminal. She was an LPG tanker built in 1996 and registered in Singapore. She has since been sold to shipping interests in Monaco.

Sai Kung
14,811 grt

A fine looking general cargo ship coming into the Bull Anchorage on 13 June 1997, with her port anchor walked out and ready for dropping. *Sai Kung* was built in 1978 at the Piel yard, Jurong, China. She was registered in Hong Kong and is named after a particularly pretty island.

Borelly
571 grt

A familiar visitor to the Humber was this well-found little coaster. *Borelly* is here in the western entrance to the Bull Channel, outward bound from Hessle Haven, on 28 August 1997. She was built in 1971 by Scheepswerf G. Bijlsma, Wartena and is owned and operated by Genchem Marine.

Torril Knutsen
14,190 dwt

With her sister ship, the *Pascale Knutsen*, *Torril Knutsen* is a regular caller at the Immingham Oil Terminal and was seen here on 15 August 1997 in the Bull Channel. Construction was by Juliana, Constr Gijonesa, in 1990. She is described as an oil/chemical tanker and is owned by Knutsen OAS Shipping AS and registered in Haugesund.

Impulsive   A day fishing vessel operating out of Grimsby and owned by Northeast Coast Charter Boats, *Impulsive* is available for trips ranging from 12 to 38 hours. Originally built as an inshore fishing vessel, she was refitted for day fishing, and is regularly seen in the estuary. This photograph was taken on 14 December 1997.

Foylebank

18,663 grt
22,911 dwt

Seen in the Bull Channel inward bound for Hull on 26 September 1997, the Isle of Man-registered *Foylebank* was one of a trio of vessels obtained by Andrew Weir & Co Ltd (Bank Line) in 1995 from Russian operators. The three – *Foylebank* (ex-*Tiksi*), *Speybank* (ex-*Okha*) and *Teighnbank* (ex-*Nikel*) – along with the *Forthbank*, operated Weir's South Pacific service. In 2006, *Foylebank* was renamed *Gazellebank* following a refit.

Bardsey

1,144 grt

Once a regular visitor to the estuary and River Humber, this well-maintained little vessel appears to have a minimal freeboard. On 28 October 1997, she was spotted in the Bull Channel outward bound from the Immingham Oil Terminal. The ship was built in 1981, and was owned and operated by Crescent Marine Ltd. She was registered in London but has since been sold to Turkish interests.

Selectivity

A general cargo vessel owned by F.T. Everard Ltd of London. She is seen here in the Bull Anchorage, fully laden and with a deck cargo of timber, on 27 October 1997.

Daniella

5,818 grt
7,580 dwt

Jumbo Navigation NV, otherwise known as *Jumboship*, specialise in providing a variety of heavy lift vessels. *Daniella* is seen in the Humber Estuary heading for the Bull Anchorage on 27 December 1997. She was built in 1989 and is designated an E-type heavy lift ship. Each individual derrick can lift 250 tonnes, and together they can lift a maximum of 650 tonnes.

Boracay

21,213 grt

In this photograph, taken on 27 December 1997, she is seen passing Spurn Point inwards for Immingham as part of the Olsen Lines service between Immingham and the continent. She was built in 1978 by AB Oskarshamns Varv, Oskarshamn. She experienced a number of name and owner changes before becoming the *Boracay* in 1987.

Ibn al Abbar

15,455 grt
23,618 dwt

The United Arab Shipping Co Ltd (SAG) has a large fleet of well-found, well-maintained cargo and cellular container vessels of which the *Ibn al Abbar* is a good example. She is one of a large number of 175m loa, 24m beam, 16 knot general cargo vessels built for UAS in the mid-1970s. She is seen passing the Spurn Point end, inwards for Hull, on 27 April 1998.

Lady Debbie

Bollard pull: 50 tonnes

She is photographed here in the Bull Anchorage waiting to assist with the berthing of the tanker, *Bergina*, at the Tetney Monobuoy on 7 May 1998. Owned by Howard Smith Towage, she was built in 1978 by Cochranes of Selby. Although mainly used in the docks and estuary she also operated in coastal work and short sea voyages.

Fast Ann

1,740 grt
1,900 dwt

A fine-looking coastal vessel, *Fast Ann* is pictured here in the western end of the Bull Channel on 7 May 1998. She was built in 1980, making her 18 years old at the time of the photograph. She appears to be wearing well! Registered in Vanuatu, she was owned by Polish Baltic Shipping, Kolobrzeg and operated by Fast Line Shipping.

Geest Merchant
2,899 dwt

Geest Line has operated a regular container service between Hull, other Humber ports and the near continent for many years. With a capacity of 340 TEU, *Geest Merchant* is a good example of the useful size feeder container vessels used by the company. She is shown here approaching the Cleeness in the Bull Channel on 25 April 1998. Built in 1995 by Elbewerft Boizenburg, she was owned by Jorg Koping Shipping Co and operated by Geest North Sea Line.

Skyman
12,612 grt
17,100 dwt

A general cargo vessel with heavy lift capability at either No. 2 or No. 3 hatch, *Skyman* is typical of the type of vessel built in the 1970s. Her owners were Transman Shipping Enterprises, SA, Athens, and she was registered in Cyprus. Pictured here on 21 April 1998, she was sold to Bangladeshi shipbreakers eight years later, in 2006.

Arnafell   *Arnafell* is another good example of the modern geared feeder container vessel. She is seen here in the Bull Channel outwards from Hull to Reykjavik on 7 April 1998, a misty day. The ship was built in 1994 by Orskov Staalskibsvaerft, Frederikshavn, Denmark and operated by Samskip. She had a capacity of 340 TEU.

HMS Shetland   The Island Class Offshore Patrol Vessel, HMS *Shetland*, was a regular visitor to Grimsby and is seen here leaving the lock to go to her berth under the care of the tug, *Jadi*, on 1 April 1998. All seven members of the Isles Class were built by Hall Russell & Co Ltd, Aberdeen, and were commissioned between October 1976 and October 1979. Though operating under Captain Fishery Protection Squadron jurisdiction, the Isles Class could also be deployed to protect oil production platforms and oil rigs in the northern North Sea and the Norwegian Sea.

At 925 tonnes (standard) and 1260 tonnes (full load), the Isles Class were powered by Ruston RKCM 12-cylinder diesels, giving a maximum speed of 16.5 knots. Their maximum range was 7000 miles at 12 knots.

Ebro

2,238 grt
2,898 dwt

A double-hull chemical tanker with stainless steel tanks built in 1986 by Wartsila. On 30 March 1998 she was inward bound for Salt End Jetty and is seen in the Bull Channel. Her port of registry was Maderia.

Cem Clipper
2,498 grt

Lying in the Bull Anchorage on 24 March 1998 was this rather unusual vessel, a bulk cement carrier with self-discharging gear. *Cem Clipper* was built in 1971 by Honda Zosen KK, Saiki, Japan. Registered in St. Vincent, her owners were Cem Bulk Carriers.

Cherry Sand
1,080 grt

This vessel is always busy around the ports of the Lower and Upper Humber. Built in 1968 by Appledore Shipbuilders, Devon, *Cherry Sand* was 30 years old when this photograph was taken on 25 March 1998. She is seen here in Grimsby Middle. She is described as a self-propelled grab hopper dredger. *Cherry Sand* was extensively modified in 1994, and then again in 1999, and continues to give her owners, United Kingdom Dredging (a division of Associated British Ports), good service.

Arco Avon
3,437 grt

Ploughing her way down the Bull Channel is this trailing suction hopper dredger. *Arco Avon* is owned by Hansen Marine Aggregates, and was built in 1986 by Appledore Ferguson Shipbuilders, Appledore, Devon. She is seen here on 5 March 1998.

Seki Cedar
1,1861 grt
7,354 dwt

Here is an unlovely but hard-working vessel! Seen on 5 March 1998 in the Bull Channel, she is inward bound for Grimsby Alexandra Dock with a cargo of cars. She was built in 1978 by Kegoya Dock KK, Kure, Japan. Described as a Ro-Ro/Container ship, she has a capacity of 900 cars and is owned by Vega Reederi Freedrich Dauber KG, Hamburg.

Short Sea Trader

2,236 grt

Steaming down the Bull Channel in a fairly light condition on 10 February 1998, is the *Short Sea Trader*, built by Cochrane of Selby in 1991. She has since been renamed *Union Saturn*.

Erna A coaster with a deck cargo of timber lies in the Bull Anchorage on 20 July 1998 waiting for the tide discharge at one of the upper Humber ports.

Linda Buck

2,295 grt
2,596 dwt

Providing a feeder container service between European ports and Goole, Seawheel operated *Linda Buck*, and a similar vessel called the *Rolf Buck*. They were built in 1995 in Germany and had a capacity of 180 TEU. They were unusual looking vessels; described as general dry cargo/Ro-Ro/container ships, they also had a stern door and ramp. This photograph was taken on 21 June 1998.

Lagarfoss

Emskip provides a feeder container service between Humber ports and Iceland by means of a number of ships of the type shown here.

On 7 June 1998, the *Bakkafoss* was waiting in the Bull Anchorage for a berth while her sister ship, the *Lagarfoss* passed Spurn Point, outward bound. Both vessels were built by J.J. Sietas KG, Schiffswerft GmbH & Co, Hamburg; one in 1983 and the other in 1982, and were registered in Antigua. *Lagarfoss* was owned by Lagar Line Ltd, and *Bakkafoss* was owned by Bakka Line Ltd.

Borussia Dortmund

6,362 grt
7,050 dwt

Named after the famous football club and apparently in their colours, this smart Feeder Container vessel lies in the Bull Anchorage on 29 May 1998 awaiting a berth in Hull. She was built by J.J. Sietas KG Schiffswerft, Hamburg, in 1998 and was brand new when this photograph was taken. She has a capacity of 700 TEU. Registered in St Johns, she is owned by Reederei Rudolf Schepers Haren/Ems and operated by ESF Euroservices.

James Clark Ross

5,731 grt

The Antarctic oceanographic ship, *James Clark Ross*, was launched at Swan Hunter by HM Queen Elizabeth II on 1 December 1990. Built to replace the aging *John Biscoe*, she was handed over to the British Antarctic Survey in 1991 and is registered in Port Stanley, Falkland Isles. She is seen here in Grimsby Roads on 16 June 1998, shortly after her return from the South Atlantic.

Heading inwards at the seaward
end of the Bull Channel on the
evening of 11 February 2000.

Multitank Bracaria
3,726 grt
5,846 dwt

Only a year old when seen in the Bull Anchorage on 19 May 1998, *Multitank Bracaria* was owned by Ahrenkill Ship Management. An chemical/oil product carrier, she was built in 1997 by Estaleiros Navios de Viana do Castelo, Viana do Castelo, Portugal. She is registered in Liberia and has since changed to *Bow Bracaria*.

Englishman

1,501 grt
Bollard pull: 132 tonnes

An icebreaking/supply AHT, the *Englishman* is seen in the Bull Anchorage on 3 May 1998, between North Sea towing jobs. In 1995 she had been bought by Paragon Offshore Ltd, Hull and when the photograph was taken she was managed by Specialist Marine Services of Hull. She was built in 1975 by Elsflether Werft AG at Elsfleth, and is registered at Nassau.

Lady Susan

285 grt
Bollard pull: 32 tonnes

Showing the colours of the owner, Howard Smith Towage, *Lady Susan* is seen in Grimsby Roads approaching the Royal Dock Basin on 19 November 1999. The vessel is a tractor tug built in 1984 by Cochrane Shipbuilders of Selby.

Lady Stephanie

285 grt
Bollard pull: 32 tonnes

Like her sister ship, the *Lady Susan*, this 1984-built tractor tug is also approaching the Royal Dock Basin on 19 November 1999, in the Howard Smith Towage colours.

Autorunner

9,693 grt

Seen here on 26 August 1998, building up to her 20-knot sea speed in the Humber Estuary with Spurn Point in the background, the *Autorunner* heads for Bremen after discharging her 1060 cars at Alexandra Dock, Grimsby. She was built in 1994 by Bratvaag Skipsverft AS and is registered at Fredricia. She is owned by United European Car Carriers.

Al Mubarakiah
23,618 dwt

A general cargo vessel owned by the United Arab Shipping Co Ltd (SAG) seen in the Bull Anchorage on 3 November 1998 after discharging in Hull. She was built in 1974 and registered in Saudi Arabia.

Sea Devil
32,250 dwt

The owner of this vessel, Carl Buttner of Germany, has many other similar tankers which are regularly seen in the Humber. The *Sea Devil* is an oil/product tanker built in 1996 by Lindenau Shipyard, Germany. She is shown passing Spurn Point on 20 October 1998.

Antares
19,963 grt

Built by the Gdansk Shipyard, Gdanskissa, Poland, she has a capacity of 41 TEU. Her owners, the Finnlines Group Ltd used her for a while on the Immingham–Rotterdam service. On 7 February 1999 was seen passing Spurn Point into the teeth of a 50 knot north-easterly gale.

STM Atria

Originally built as a stern trawler, the *Othsmarschen*, in Germany in 1965, she was operating as an offshore/ ROV support vessel when this photograph was taken on 23 May 1999. At the time she was engaged in a pipeline survey in the Humber Estuary. She was owned by Yeomen Shipping Ltd. and operated by DSND SeaTeam. In 2003 she was broken up at Grenaa, Denmark.

Jacobus Broere
5,098 dwt

With the BP production plant on the north bank of the Humber and two oil refineries on the south bank, the estuary is busy with vessels of this type. She is a 1989-built chemical/oil tanker and is seen here on 12 June 1999 in the Bull Anchorage waiting for a berth upriver. The vessel was built at the Shipyard de Hoop, Netherlands, featured stainless steel tanks, and was owned by Gebr Broere DV, Dordrecht.

Tim Rix
1,987 grt

Taken on 24 May 1999, the picture shows *Tim Rix* heading for the Bull Anchorage to find a spot to await further instructions. Together with her sister ship the *Jonrix*, *Tim Rix* was a regular run from Hull to Estonian ports bringing in timber, as can be seen from her deck cargo. *Tim Rix* belongs to J.R. Rix & Sons of Hull, and was built in 1977 by Imamura Zosen, Kure, Japan. She has a capacity of 105 TEU.

Butt   An oil product tanker in the Bull Channel heading seawards from the Immingham Oil Terminal on 10 March 1999.

Thor Scan
7,991 grt
9,800 dwt

A general cargo/container vessel with two cranes which each have a 50-tonne capacity, *Thor Scan* was in the Bull Anchorage when this photograph was taken on 5 March 1999. Built in 1982 by Schiffswerft Martin Jansen, Leer, she is owned by Thor Scan Shipping NV, Willemstad, and is registered in that city. At the time of the photograph, she was managed by Mammoet Transport, Amsterdam.

Ramform Victory
10,297 grt

An unusual-looking Seismic Research Vessel, *Ramform Victory* was built in 1998 by Langsten Slip Batbyggeri AS. At the time, she was owned by the government of Japan but operated by PGS Geophysical AS, Norway. She is registered in Bergen. She is pictured on 22 February 1999 coming into the Humber Estuary to find shelter from the 50-knot north-easterly gale blowing at the time.

Tideway Rollingstone
11,502 grt

Described simply as a *Rock Dumping Vessel*, she was originally built as the semi-submersible, *Super Servant 1* in 1979 by Oshima Shipbuilding Co Ltd, Sumitomo, Japan. In 1994 she was sold to Tideway BV (Dredging International NV), Breda and sent to YVC Bolnes of Rotterdam to be converted. She emerged as a Rock Dumping Vessel and was registered in Cyprus. She is shown here on 21 February 1999 in the Humber Estuary.

Sand Heron
3,751 grt

Heading for sea in the Humber Estuary is this aggregate dredger. She is a trailing suction hopper dredger, built in 1990 by the Merwede Shipyard BV for the South Coast Shipping Co Ltd of Southampton. She has a capacity of 2,500m^3. She was operating for RMC Marine when the photograph was taken on 8 February 1999.

Anne Mieke

8,388 grt
9,549 dwt

Anne Mieke is a Type 161 three-hatch heavy lift vessel. Two of her cranes are rated at 275 tonnes, and the other at 150 tonnes. She is pictured here in the Bull Anchorage on 28 September 1999. The ship was built in 1998 by J.J. Sietas KG Schiffswerft GmbH & Co, and owned by SAL Transport Gmbh, Hamburg.

Lani

1,600 grt

The *Lani* crosses the Bull Anchorage inward bound for Grimsby on 21 September 1999. She is one of a class known as Russian River Ships and was built in 1978 by the Finnish yard Rauma Reola Savailinna, Nystad. At the time of the photograph she was owned by the North Western Shipping Co.

Rossini
2,195 grt
2,750 dwt

Under way on 8 September 1999 in the Bull Channel with a strong south-westerly wind blowing is this product of the Damen Shipyard BV. She was built in 1998 for Oceanflag Shipping Ltd, registered in Limassol, and was managed by GEFO - Gesellschaft Fur Oeltransporte mbH.

Mekhanik Fomin
2,489 grt
2,654 dwt

Here we see a unitised timber carrier in the Bull Anchorage on 24 July 1999 waiting for a berth at Freshney Place, Grimsby. She was built in 1991 and is owned by N.S.C. of Archangel.

Skiropoula
68,232 dwt

An oil product tanker passing Spurn Point on 19 July 1999, *Skiropoula* appears to be in loaded condition and outwards from Immingham Oil Terminal. The vessel was built in 1995 by the Zaliv Shipyard, Ukraine and is owned by the Greek, Eletson Corporation.

Agila
1,418 grt
4,530 dwt

PAL Line Services provide a Feeder Container service between European ports and Hull and Goole. Here the *Agila* is seen in the Bull Channel, inwards for Hull on 21 July 1999. She was built in 1995 at the Sitas Shipyard in Hamburg. The owners were Transatlantic European Services AB and she was operated by PAL Line. Her capacity is 304 TEU, and her port of registry is Antigua.

Kildin
684 grt

An unusual visitor to Grimsby on 12 July 1999 was this general cargo/multipurpose vessel. *Kildin* was one of a class of ships from the Russian Black Sea fleet which also had the reputation of being spy ships, thanks to her large number of radio aerials! She was built in 1988, and owned by Ardistelo Ltd. In the photograph she is seen in Grimsby Roads, with a pilot on board, making her approach to Grimsby Royal Dock Basin.

Feeder Pilot
9,933 grt

Built for capacity and not for looks, *Feeder Pilot* is a familiar sight in the Humber and in Grimsby. She has since been renamed as *Neckar Highway*, but at the time this picture was taken, on 25 August 1999, she was operated by E.H. Harms importing and exporting 850 cars at a time between Ems and Grimsby. *Feeder Pilot* was built earlier that year by Hegemann Rolandwerft, Keil, registered at Limassol, and was owned by P.D. Gram and Co.

UKD Bluefin

4,171 grt

A modern trailing suction dredger owned by UKD Dredging – part of ABP Ltd – pictured here operating in the vicinity of Tetney Monobuoy on 11 August 1999. She was built by Ferguson Shipbuilders at Port Glasgow in 1997.

The company was originally founded in 1903 on a somewhat restricted site west of Newark Castle which limited the length of ships built there to around 300ft. The yard became part of the Lithgow group in 1963, and later nationalised into British Shipbuilders in 1977. From 1981–86 it was linked with the Ailsa shipyard at Troon, forming Ferguson Ailsa Ltd, and when the arrangement broke up, there followed a three-year tryst with Appledore Shipbuilders Ltd, Bideford, Devon. This arrangement also failed to work out, and in 1989, the yard was sold to Clark-Kincaid to become Fergusson (Kvaerner Govan) Ltd.

In 1991, the yard changed hands for the fifth time since the end of the Second World War, when it was bought by Ferguson Marine. The name was changed to Ferguson Shipbuilders Ltd, and massive restructuring and investment in such areas such as computer-aided design and computer-aided manufacturing saw the yard transformed into a profit-making business.

Loverval

10,931 grt

Owned by Cobelfret Ferries NV, *Loverval* provided a Ro-Ro service between Immingham and Zeebrugge from 1983 to 2003. The vessel was built in 1978 by Lodose Varv AB, Lodose. She is seen here passing Spurn Point on the evening of 16 August 1999. In 2003 she was sold by Cobelfret and renamed *Marabou*.

Aquamarine

3,080 grt

1,120 dwt

Aquamarine is a diving support vessel built in 1981 by Oy Wartsila AB and owned by DSND Subsea Ltd. Since this photograph was taken on 11 August 1999, she has since had various changes of name and is now owned by Bibby under the name *Bibby Aquamarine* and is owned by Bibby. Here she is shown working in the Humber Estuary in the vicinity of the Tetney Monobuoy.

Heerebrug
2,035 grt
2,850 dwt

This is an example of the kind of feeder container vessel which is used to provide container services between Goole and the continent. *Heerebrug* was built by Frisian Welgelegen Scheepswerft in 1999. She is owned by Armawa Shipping & Trading BV and is registered in the Netherlands. The picture shows her on 29 September 1999 in the Bull Channel.

Stolt Dipper
3,206 grt
4,750 dwt

The *Stolt Dipper*, lying to her port anchor in the Bull Anchorage, on 11 November 1999. This vessel is owned by Stolt Nielsen SA, and was built in 1992 by Aarhus Dockyards, Denmark.

Amenity
1,696 grt

Another ship from the fleet of F.T. Everard and Sons Ltd, *Amenity* is pictured in the Bull Anchorage on 28 October 1999 before their merger with James Fisher. She was built in 1980 by the Goole Shipbuilding Co Ltd, and since this picture was taken, has been sold and renamed *Unicom Energy*.

Pasewalk
4,961 grt

Taken in the evening of 29 Septmber 2000, this picture shows the 1983-built Ro-Ro in the Bull Channel, outwards from Immingham. *Pasewalk* was built by Veb Mathias-Thesen-Werft, is owned by Reederi F. Laeisz GmbH and operated by Cargo Connected Transport. She is registered in Liberia.

Rossnes
3,883 grt

Wilson ships are often seen in the estuary and here their Valetta-registered bulk carrier *Rossnes* is pictured in the Bull Anchorage on 17 August 2000. Built in 1975 by Eide Contracting her owners were Wilson Shipowning and managers Wilson Ship Management. She was later renamed *Wilson Ross*.

Furenas
8,930 grt
12,724 dwt

The fine-looking Swedish-registered chemical/oil tanker, *Furenas*, lying in the Bull Anchorage on 19 December 2000. At the time she was just two years old, having been built in 1998 by Soviknes Verft AS, Soviknes, Norway. She is owned by Furetank Rederi AS.

Silver Stream
263 grt

Silver Stream was an immaculate Grimsby-registered long line fishing vessel built in 1998 in Norway. She is seen here leaving Grimsby Fish Dock on 8 August 2000. This beautiful looking vessel had a sad ending in 2004 when she caught fire while on the slip in Grimsby Fish Dock. Although the fire was extinguished by the Fire Service, the resulting damage meant that the ship was a total loss.

Rix Harrier
572 grt
1,009 dwt

In 1996 J.&R. Rix Shipping of Hull bought the *Rix Harrier*, which had been built in 1979 by the Yorkshire Dry Dock Co Ltd, Hull, and had her converted to a bunker vessel. The conversion was carried out by the Hepworth Shipyard, Paull, East Yorkshire, and included the fitting of two Caterpillar main engines. The photograph, taken on 9 August 2000, shows her approaching the *Navion Anglia* in the Humber Estuary to bunker her.

Aldrington
6,570 dwt

A bulk carrier built in 1978 by Mbtar-Nauta, Sp-Zoo, Gdinya, Poland, *Aldrington* was owned by Continental Shipmanagement AS, Norway. In this photograph, taken on 18 April 2000, part of Spurn Point, including the tower housing Spurn Pilots and VTS Humber can be seen in the background as well the Humber lifeboat at her moorings.

Tarquin Loch
4,963 grt

The Panama-registered LPG tanker, *Tarquin Loch*, shown at speed in the Bull Channel on 24 May 2000, having cleared Immingham Gas Terminal after loading. She was built by Hyundai Heavy Industries, Korea, and owned by the Liquid Gas Shipping.

Wear Fisher

3,120 dwt

The *Wear Fisher* in the Humber Estuary in loaded condition on 9 February 2000. She was built in 1980 by the Appledore Shipbuilding Co Ltd, Appledore, Devon, and was owned by James Fisher & Co Ltd, Barrow-in-Furness. Fisher's has since sold her and she has been renamed *Venus*.

HMS York

The Royal Navy often makes visits to ports on the Humber and opens its vessels to the public. Here, on 26 June 2000, the Type 42 destroyer HMS *York* is seen passing Spurn Point outwards from a visit to Hull. HMS *York* is one of four Batch 3 Type 42s – the others are HM ships *Manchester, Gloucester* and *Edinburgh*. The completion of these four ships was delayed so that modifications resulting from experience in the Falklands campaign could be incorporated.

Powered by two Rolls-Royce Olympus TM3B gas turbines for full power and two Rolls-Royce Tyne RMIC gas turbines for cruising, the Batch 3 Type 42s are capable of 30+ knots when necessary and have a range of 4000 miles at 18 knots. *York* was laid down at Swan Hunter on 18 January 1980, launched on 21 June 1982 and commissioned on 9 August 1985.

HMS Coventry

The Broadsword Class Type 22 guided missile frigate, HMS *Coventry*, heads for sea on 9 February 2000. She was one of six Batch 2 Type 22s, and was laid down at Swan Hunter on 29 March 1984. This was a unique day at Swan Hunter as the Keel of the HMS *Sheffield* was also laid down; both ships replacing the Type 42 destroyers *Coventry* and *Sheffield* which were lost during the Falklands campaign.

The new *Coventry* was launched on 6 April 1986, and commissioned on 14 October 1988. Powered by two Rolls-Royce Olympus TM3B high-speed gas turbines, and two Rolls-Royce Tyne RMIC cruise gas turbines, *Coventry* had a range of 8.000 miles. She displaced 4.800 tons, 146.5m loa, beam 14.8m, draught 6.4m, and carried a complement of 273. Decommissioned on 17 January 2002, she was sold to the Romanian Navy on 14 January 2003 and renamed *Regele Ferdinand*.

Moldavia and RMS Arcturus

Moldavia:	1,546 grt
	1,708 dwt
Arcturus:	1,864 grt
	2,517 dwt

Two vessels managed by Rhein-Maas Shipping pass in the Humber Estuary on 19 December 2000. The *Moldavia* was built in 1985 by Peterswerft Wewelsfleth GmbH & Co, Wewelsfleth, Germany in 1985 and owned by Schiffinvest GmbH Co KG. She was later renamed RMS *Wedau*. *Arcturus* was built by ATG, Actur Shipping Co. Her capacity was 105 TEU.

Ugglegorsk
3,936 grt
4,168 dwt

This single-deck general cargo vessel had just arrived from the port of Galatz on 29 September 2001, and was in the Bull Anchorage awaiting a berth in Grimsby. She was built in 1990 by Sedef Gemi Endudstisi SA, Turkey and owned by Unicom Lines (Pty), Durban. Her container capacity is 224 TEU.

Hoopride
794 grt
1,394 dwt

Sadly, no longer operating, R. Lapthorn ships used to be regularly sights in the estuary. Here, the *Hoopride* is in the Bull Anchorage on 7 June 2001. She was built in 1984 by the Yorksire Dry Dock Co Ltd, Hull. Although operated by Lapthorns, the vessel was owned by John I. Jacobs PLC of London.

Brae Trader

44,989 grt
89,730 dwt

Brae Trader was a standard Crude tanker built in 1975 by the Oshima Shipbuilding Co, Nagasaki, Japan, and originally named *Hellespont Pride*. Owned by the Braer Corporation, Monrovia, and managed by BeH Ship Management, USA, she is pictured here in the Humber Estuary on 20 April 1986. Later renamed *Braer*, she gained everlasting infamy when she grounded on Sumburgh Head, Shetland, spilling all her cargo into the sea. The tug is the *Lady Sarah*.

Spirit of Scotland

A gaff-rigged schooner built between 1981 and 1985 by the Merseyside Trust, she is an exact replica of a Victorian Liverpool Bay Pilot Cutter. Seen here entering the Bull Channel on 30 August 1997 she was circumnavigating Britain during that summer. Originally built as the *Spirit of Fairbridge*, her name was changed when Scottish Nuclear became her sponsors. At 92ft long, she can accommodate 12 young people on training/adventure cruises, and her home port is Dundee where she is open to the public.

Seillean

This a dynamically positioned, self-propelled deepwater FPSO (Floating, Production, Storage and Off-loading). She is designed to connect to and produce crude oil from deep sub-sea oil wells without the need for off-shore support vessels. *Seillean*, whose name means 'honeybee' in Gaellic, was designed by BP and Harland & Wolff, and built by Harland & Wolff Ltd, Belfast in 1987. She displaces 76,440 tonnes when full.

A designated a SWOPS vessel (Single Well Oil Production System), BP employed her on the Cyrus oil field and then the Donan field, both in the North Sea. The photograph shows her in the Humber Estuary, approaching Tetney Monobuoy with a cargo of Donan crude on 5 May 1994, when she was being operated by Redding & Bates. She remained active in the North Sea until 1997 when she went to work on Brazilian oil fields.

Kula

4,446 grt
6,260 dwt

Seen in the Bull Anchorage on 25 August 1998, *Kula* is a Turkish built and owned general cargo vessel. Built in 1987 at Camialti, Istanbul, her main engine was built in the Netherlands by Stork Werkspoor. The owners at the time were Turkish Cargo Lines Ltd.

Christine Nielsen GY298
147 grt

Looking in good shape for a 1975-built fishing vessel, *Christine Nielsen* is seen here having just left Grimsby Fish Dock on 2 August 1998. Built in Denmark, she was owned by a partnership in North Shields.

Humber Callisto

At the time this photograph was taken, on 28 September 2000, this was the latest addition to the ABP Pilot Launch fleet. *Humber Callisto* was built by Canmarc Ltd, Souler Marine, Cowes, and is owned by ABP Ltd, Hull. She is a 56ft Pilot Launch with a water-jet propulsion which gives her a top speed of 37 knots.

Magdeline Anne
SH33 & Crusader of Kingswear DH71

These two inshore fishing vessels are seen off Cleeness in the Bull Channel heading for Grimsby Fish Dock on 22 February 2000. *Magdeline Anne* is registered in Scarborough and was built in 1960 at Girvan. She is 18 tonnes. The *Crusader of Kingswear* is registered at Dartmouth. She was built in 1976 at Appledore and is 44 tonnes.

Saroya GY376 This Grimsby 'Snibby' (local parlance for a Seine Net Fishing vessel) is pictured on 6 April 2000 having left Grimsby Fish Dock for the North Sea. *Saroya* was built in Denmark in 1957 and is 45 tons, with power of 243kW.

Pesha An elderly Russian stern trawler, built in 1977, *Pesha* is seen here in Grimsby Roads Approaching
395 dwt Grimsby Royal Dock Basin on 3 October 2001.

Eberhard
3,075 frt
5,235 dwt

A smart looking German owned chemical/oil product tanker in the Bull Channel, outwards from the Immingham Oil Terminal on 25 October 2001. Registered in Antigua, she was built in 1983 by Kroger Werft Rendsburg Gmbh. She was owned by Reederei TMS *Eberhard* GmbH & Co and managed by Carl F. Peters Gmbh & Co KG.

Arneb
3,640 grt

This is the *Arneb* on 28 October 2001, having just returned from taking plutonium from Dounreay, Scotland, to Germany. Built in Hamburg in 1986, and classified INF2 (Irradiated Nuclear Fuel) by Lloyds Register, *Arneb* spent most of her time transporting plutonium around Europe. It wasn't without controversy; Greenpeace protested that she was unsuitable because of her single hull. Owned by International Nuclear Services and operated by the Nuclear Decommissioning Authority, she was later renamed *Atlantic Osprey*.

Victoria Pride
16,794 grt
24,232 dwt

Owned by the Pacifica Navigation Co Ltd, this Malta registered bulk carrier was in the Bull Anchorage on 10 November 2001 waiting for a berth in Immingham Docks. She was built in 1985.

Patricia Essberger
2,557 grt
4,711 dwt

Patricia Essberger was a new ship when this photograph of her was taken on 15 November 2001 in the Bull Anchorage. The chemical tanker was built in 2000 by J.J. Sietas of Hamburg and owned by Broere Shipping.

Lystind
4,471 grt
3,700 dwt

Classed as a general cargo vessel, the *Lystind* is pictured in the Bull Channel on 11 December 2001, outwards from Immingham to Norway. She was built in 1990 by Brodogradiliste Titvo, was owned by Ross Line KS and managed by DFDS Lys Line AS. She has a capacity of 56 TEU.

Crystalwater
1,655 grt
2,983 dwt

A chemical tanker built in 1997, *Crystalwater* is pictured here at anchor in the Bull Anchorage on 25 September 2001, waiting for the tide to go to Gunness on the River Trent. She is owned by the Clearwater group, Papendrecht.

Tor Humbria

20,165 grt
14,763 dwt

Steaming down the Bull Channel on 18 August 2001 outwards from Immingham is this 1978 built Ro-Ro operated by DFDS Tor Line Ltd. She was built by Oskarshamns Varv, Oskarshamn, Sweden. Originally built for the Middle East trade she has been operated by Tor Line since 1999.

Humber Endeavour

381 grt
650 dwt

A bunkering vessel regularly seen all around the ports of the Lower Humber, the *Humber Endeavour* is owned by John H. Whitaker Ltd of Hull, where she is registered. She was built in 1981. In the photograph she is approaching Grimsby Royal Dock Basin on 27 August 2001.

Amandine

14,094 dwt

Passing Spurn Point outwards for Rotterdam from Immingham on 17 August 2001 is this Cobelfret Ferries Ro-Ro. She was built in 1978 at the Lindenau yard, Kiel, with a capacity of 130 trailers. In 2003 she was sold and renamed *Amanda*.

Sarah

1,578 grt

A general cargo vessel built in 1978, the *Sarah* is regularly seen in the Humber. She is pictured here lying in the Bull Anchorage on 31 August 2001, bound for Goole from Tallinen.

Hoburgen
9,080 grt

This Ro-Ro vessel is seen passing Spurn Point on the evening of 28 May 2001 bound for Zeebrugge from Immingham while on a Cobelfret Ferries Charter. She was built in 1986 by Santieral Naval Galati, Romania, as *Balder Ra* and laid up until 1988 when she was bought by Rederi Ab Gotland.

Mangen
2,580 grt
3,175 dwt

A smart little geared general cargo vessel, the *Mangen* is seen here in the Bull Channel heading for Rochester from Hull on 12 August 2001. She was built in 1984 by the Nieuwe Noord Ned. Scheepswerven BV, Groningen, Netherlands, and owned by Barker Ship Management AS, Norway. At the time, she was registered in Curacao. She has since been renamed *Alholmen*.

Ladoga 11
1,510 dwt

With a deck cargo of timber this sea/river vessel is heading up the Bull Channel for Grimsby from Riga on 17 July 2001. She is owned by Estonian Ship Management, Tallinn and was built in 1973 by Laivateollisuus Turku, Resposaaren Kon, Finland.

Weser Importer
7,580 dwt

For a short period during 2000 and 2001 *Weser Importer* provided a container service between Grimsby and Norway. She is seen here, on 8 August 2001, in the Bull Anchorage waiting for the tide to enter Grimsby Royal Dock. Built in 1986 by Bremer Vulkan, Bremer-Vegesack and owned by Wesser Schiffahrts POB, Bremen, she was renamed *Normed Antwerp* in 2003.

Northern Lindnes

2,446 grt
3,710 dwt

As the writing on the ship clearly shows, this bulk carrier is managed by Wilson Ship Management, Bergen. She was built in 1997 by Slovenske Lodenice AS, Komarno, Slovakia and is owned by Jebsens Ship Management, Bergen. She was seen in the Bull Anchorage on 7 September 2001.

Clementine

23,986 grt
9,655 dwt

Yet another of the many vessels operated by the Belgian company, Soc Cobelfrett Ferries, from Immingham to near European ports, *Zeebrugge* is pictured in the Humber Estuary on 2 August 2001. She was built in 1997 by Kawasaki Heavy Industries Ltd, Sakaide, Japan, is owned by Novomar SA, Luxembourg and is registered in Belgium.

Tor Selandia
24,196 grt
11,089 dwt

A superb example of the futuristic second-generation Ro-Ro vessels built by Fincantieri Ancona, Italy for DFDS Tor Line. *Tor Selandia* was built in 1998 and has a capacity of 200 trailers. She presently operates on the Immingham–Denmark service. The photograph was taken on 4 September 2001 as the vessel approached Spurn Point, outwards for Denmark.

Bro Nelly
5,767 dwt

A chemical tanker built in 1997 by Union Naval de Levante SA, Spain, for Brostrom Tankers AB, Sweden. (United Tankers). In 2003 she was sold to Wonsild's and renamed *Clipper Nelly*. On 4 August 2001 she was seen heading inwards for Salt End to load.

Voe Venture
71 grt
Bollard pull: 13 tonnes

Typical of the variety of shipping seen in the Humber is this Pontoon Category 2 Workboat seen on 4 August 2001. Built in 1984 by Damen Shipyard, Hardinxveld, Dordrecht, she is owned by Delta Marine of Lerwick in Shetland. The vessel has a maximum lift crane of 100 tonnes.

Odergas
4,201 grt
4,000 dwt

At only two years old when this picture was taken, on 25 September 2001, *Odergas* looks smart as she proceeds down the Bull Channel. Built in 1999, she is owned by Hartmann Reederi, Germany, and operated by GasChem. The vessel is an LPG carrier built by Severnov SA, Turnu Severin, Romania. She is registered in Monrovia.

Navion Britannia

72,110 grt
124,821 dwt

The *Navion Britannia* is pictured here on 29 September 2001 secured to the Tetney Monobuoy, with the tug *Lady Kathleen* assisting. Built in 1998 by Astilleros Espanoles at the Sestao Yard, this 265m loa, 43m beam twin-screw tanker has a capacity of 139,500m³. Designed to load offshore, either over the bow or by Submerged Turret Loading, she can also undertake offshore oil production courtesy of her Submerged Turret Production System.

Once managed by Knutsen OAS Shipping for Navion ASA – the Norwegian government owned Statoil AS which also operates ships through Einar Rasmussen – *Navion Britannia* later moved to Teekay Shipping. The *Lady Kathleen* was built in 1991 by McTay Marine, Bromborough for Howard Smith Towage Ltd, and was equipped with two Voith propulsion units, giving her a bollard pull of 52 tonnes. She is seen here in the colours of Adstream Towing Ltd.

Lotta Kosan

2,223 grt
2,004 dwt

Lotta Kosan coming to anchor in the Bull Anchorage
on 7 June 2001. Registered in Douglas, Isle of Man, at
the time of the photograph, this LPG tanker was
owned by Lauritzen Kosan, Copenhagen, having been
built in 1992 by Sverken, Pepenburg GmbH. She was
sold to Eitzen Gas in 2006.

Miniforest

2,016 grt
22,545 dwt

Inward bound from Riga, the single-deck timber carrier *Miniforest* heads up the Bull Channel bound for Killingholme on 10 November 2001. The 1972 German-built vessel was owned by Tallship Ship Management, Tallin, Estonia.

Teesdale H

Seen here on 19 January 2002, this bunkering vessel is in the Bull Channel on her way from Immingham to bunker the tanker *Navion Hispania*. She is owned by J.H. Whitaker Ltd of Hull and is registered in Hull. She was built in 1976.

Navion Anglia

71,622 grt
126,650 dwt

The North Sea Shuttle Tanker *Navion Anglia* is another product of the Spanish yard, Astilleros Espanoles SA, and was completed in 1999. Listed in 2000 as being managed by Knutsen OAS Shipping AS for Navion ASA, when this picture was taken on 22 July 2001, she was owned by Navion Offshore Loading AS and managed by Teekay Marine Services. She is pictured here approaching the Tetney Monobuoy.

Seabass

21,353 grt
32,480 dwt

A product of the German, Lindenau GmbH Shipyard, Kiel, this oil product tanker was built in 2001 and owned by Carl Buttner/German Tanker Shipping. She is pictured here approaching Spurn Point, outward bound from the Immingham Oil Terminal on 22 January 2002.

Stena Seatrader

Seen early in the morning on 4 January 2002, the *Stena Seatrader* was inward bound for the Humber International Terminal. Owned by Stena Line BV and managed by Northern Marine Management Ltd, she was built in 1973 by Nakskov Skibsvaert, Denmark. The builders' official description of *Stena Seatrader* was that she was a car/train ferry.

Selfoss
7,676 grt
8,267 dwt

This vessel forms part of the Eimskip feeder container service between Hull and Reykjavik. She was built in 1991 by Orskov Christensen, owned by Sel Line Ltd, and at the time of the photograph, was managed by Eimskpafelag Islands ehf. She has a capacity of 724 TEU, and her port of registry is St. Johns, Antigua. Here she is seen in the Bull Channel with a good westerly blowing on 10 March 2002.

Baroy
1,926 grt
1,118 dwt

Lying to her port anchor in the Bull Anchorage, this regular visitor is awaiting a berth in Grimsby Royal Dock. The photograph was taken on 9 April 2002 when she was under charter to SeaCargo AS of Bergen. The vessel was built in 1974 by Fosen Mek. Verksteder AS, Rissa. Described as a palletized cargo ship, she is owned by Krystfrakt AS and is registered in Kingstown.

Norcape
14,087 grt

Passing Bravo Buoy, Chequer Shoal, in the Humber Estuary on the morning of 13 April 2002 is this P&O North Sea Ferries Ro-Ro, inward bound for Hull. *Norcape* was built in 1979 by the Mitsui Engineering and Ship Building Co Ltd, Taniano, Japan. She is registered in Rotterdam and owned by Norcape Shipping BV.

Vilja
9,698 grt
5,484 dwt

Pictured in the Bull Channel on 15 April 2002 is this Ro-Ro on a short-term charter to Ferryways. *Vilja* was a one-off vessel built by A. Vuyk and Zonen, Scheepswerven BV, Capelle, Holland. She is registered in Kingstown and owned by Transoceanique Suisse Compagnie de Navigation.

Futura

51,055 grt

95,195 dwt

The North Sea Shuttle Tanker *Futura* making her approach to the Tetney Monobuoy on 23 April 2002. Built at the Kvaerner Masa Yard, Turku, Finland, in 1992 for the Finnish national oil company Nestje Oyj, her design incorporated a bow loading system and a Submerged Turret Loading System. The latter system enables the 241m loa, 40m beam takner to take on cargo in some of the roughest sea and weather conditions. She was transferred with the rest of the Nestje Oyj fleet to Fortum Oyj, but was later sold to Navion Offshore and renamed *Navion Fennia*.

Norrvik

2,041 grt

3,254 dwt

A good-looking general purpose bulk carrier with a cargo of containers, *Norrvik* is pictured here on the evening of 23 April 2002, outward bound in the Humber Estuary with Spurn Point in the background. Built in 1979 by J.J. Seitas, Hamburg, she has a capacity of 134 TEU. The vessel is owned by M.V. Norrvik Shipping Ltd, Isle of Man and is registered at Douglas in the Isle of Man. When this photograph was taken she was chartered to Joensson Novabolagen AB.

Seeker

HM Customs are a necessary part of shipping business. To help the service with tracking and surveillance they purchased four specially built 40ft launches between 2000 and 2004. The *Seeker* was built in 2001 by Damen Shipyards, Gronchem, Holland, for a cost of £4m. She is seen here on 18 February 2002 in the Humber Estuary.

Teignbank
118,627 grt
22,910 dwt

Approaching Spurn Point, outwards from Hull on the first leg of the Andrew Weir Co (Bank Line) Pacific Islands service, the Finnish built *Teignbank* was one of three sisters acquired from the Russian Far East Fleet in 1995. In 2006, following a substantial refit in Singapore, she was renamed *Boularibank*. This picture was taken on 19 January 2002.

Louise Russ
18,400 grt
8,000 dwt

This modern Ro-Ro was chartered by CobelFrett Ferries for use on their Killingholme–Rotterdam service and is seen here on 2 November 2002 in the Bull Channel. She had been built in 2001 by J.J. Sietas Schiffswerft, Hamburg and is owned by Ernst Russ GmbH & Co, Hamburg, and carries 600 cars.

Sorrento GY417

Seen leaving Grimsby Fish Dock on 8 April 2002 is this Danish built 'Snibby'. She was built in 1974 and is 49 tonnes.

Seaway Commander

1,748 grt
630 dwt

Very careful examination of the profile of this vessel might reveal her history. She was built in 1967 as the Hull trawler, *Swanella* by the Goole Ship Building & Repair Co Ltd for J. Marr & Sons. Sold for use as a Diving Support vessel, she underwent major refits in 1982 and again in 1988, her names in this role being *Archimedes* and later *Dive Performer*. When pictured in the Bull Channel on 25 May 2002, she was owned by DSND Subsea and chartered to Stolt Offshore (UK).

Adventurer

The full name of this unusual looking vessel is *Cable & Wireless Adventurer*. She was built in 1998 to circumnavigate the world in less than 80 days, a feat which she successfully achieved during April, May and June of that year. Her master for the voyage was Capt. Ian Bosworth.

She was built by Vosper Thornycroft in Southampton after a design by Nigel Trens. The craft has a pencil thin centre hull and a needle thin bow and takes its basic concept from the design of the 1897 vessel *Turbina*. She is 35m loa, displaces 41 tonnes and has two 350hp Cummins turbo-diesel engines. Owned by Cable & Wireless Ltd, she was in the Bull Anchorage on 29 September 2002.

Rasmine Although built in 1972, this little 'Snibby' looks well maintained and in good condition as she leaves Grimsby Fish Dock for sea on 8 November 2002. She was built in Denmark and is 50 tonnes.

Nordic Akarita
58,928 grt
107,223 dwt

This North Sea Shuttle Tanker is shown secured to Tetney Monobuoy in the Humber Estuary on 26 November 2002. Built in 1991 by Tsuneishi Shipbuilding, she was originally known as the *Akaria*, a unit in the Ugland Capital Partner's fleet. In 1996 she became the *Stena Akria*, owned by Ugland Nordic Shipping ASA, and was registered in Liberia. When this picture was taken she was Owned by Delphine Shipping Inc and managed by Teekay Marine Services. Her port of registry was Nassau.

Grand Turk

314 grt

Based on the 1741 design for the frigate HMS *Blandford*, the Grand Turk was built in 1996 at Marmaris, Turkey. The vessel, which can carry 1050m² of sail, is said to be an authentic replica given the constraints of modern shipbuilding regulations and safety at sea (hence the inflatable dinghy at her stern).

Owned by Topsail Ships, she is available for corporate entertainment, TV and film work. She has already appeared on the small screen in the *Hornblower* and *Longitude* series. *Grand Turk* is pictured here in the Bull Anchorage on 29 May 2002.

At Heart Ltd Titles

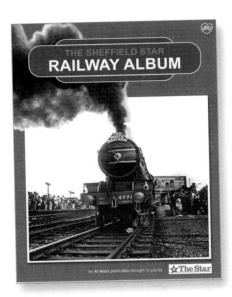

The Sheffield Star Railway Album
£14.99
ISBN: 978-184547-206-1

The Sheffield Star Railway Album takes readers on a railway tour of the surrounding area over the last century. Come with us to Sheffield Midland in the days of the LMS; see the 1500V DC electrics of the now defunct Woodhead route in action; visit Doncaster during the 1920s; and take a look at the early years of the South Yorkshire Supertram.

This album brings together readers' images with stunning photographs from *The Star*'s own archives to take you on an unmissable journey through the last hundred years of the region's railways.

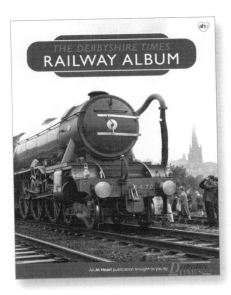

The Derbyshire Times Railway Album
£14.99
ISBN: 978-1-84547-200-9

The Derbyshire Times Railway Album is much more than just a rivet-counting railway book. It is a chance to take a closer look around Derbyshire's most distinctive trains and railways through a stunning selection of photographs from throughout the 20th century.

Containing over 200 images from libraries, readers and the *Derbyshire Times*' own extensive archives, you can get closer than ever before to all the landmark stations, principle routes and, of course, the key locomotives to travel to them.

If you would like any further information on the above titles please contact us at the address below.
At Heart Ltd: 32 Stamford Street, Altrincham, Cheshire, WA14 1EY **Tel:** 0161 924 0159 **Fax:** 0161 924 0160